The intentions of this book is to address a spectrum of human experiences through devotionals, poetry, and personal testimony. This was inspired by the Gospel of Jesus Christ. I hope that this reading shines a light over your circumstances whether they are physical, spiritual, mental, or emotional.

INTRODUCTION
The Foundation for an Abundant Life

THE CRIES OF:

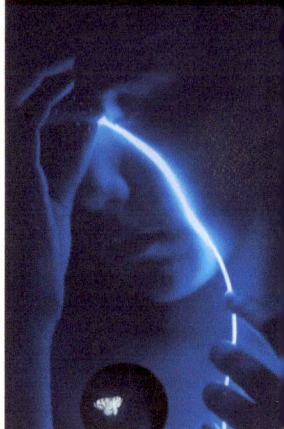

Cries of a Loved Soul

INTRODUCTION
The Foundation For An Abundant Life

Our human experience has been illustrated by mortality, despair, & fear. This reality serves as a reminder that we all need healing. Healing that requires humility & stability. Each one of us is given a separate life journey in which we discover the foundation of our existence.

The foundation of a human life consists of morals, beliefs, opinions, emotions & reactions. But what is the Foundation for a Life in Abundance?

When God descended as a Man on Earth, he laid a Strong & Infinite Foundation so that we can All Stand & Rest on. This Foundation is Jesus Christ. A Foundation of Strength, Protection, Healing, Identity, Discipline, Intimacy, Friendship, Spirituality, Peace, Humility & Eternal Life.God set this Foundation so that we aren't failing in our self-sufficiency.

For us a child is born, to us a son is given, and the government will be on his shoulders. And he will be called Wonderful Counselor, Mighty God, Everlasting Father, Prince of Peace.
Isaiah 9:6

How do I live by this Foundation?

Faith

Believe that you are a Child of God & that you are graced with infinite Love & forgiveness. Believe that you are here with a purpose and that your existence is evidence of how real & merciful God is. Through faith you become open to the infinite & rewarding guidance of Jesus Christ. His guidance manifests through the creation, our encounters with one another, difficult situations and the miracles we experience as well. You will surely know when God is speaking to you because you've allowed yourself to have a spiritual identity through the Light of Jesus.

Surrender

God is the only one aware of everything that has happened and will happen in your life. God is also aware of everything outside of humanity. He operates in the celestial & spiritual realms, where he isn't bound by space or time. When you surrender, you are allowing God to write out your story. Surrender means that you won't have all the answers but God is the victor of all things. He will give you the wisdom you need for each day and the hope to persevere in any situation. Surrender means to trust.

Love

It is said that if we don't have Love we have nothing. Our journey with Christ truly is a love story. A story of how we are redeemed, forgiven and given countless opportunities to get up. A story of how God sees us in a light opposed to how we see and carry ourselves. A story of how we are protected even in the toughest situations. A story of how we are victorious because of his faith in us, as well.

I Am The Way, The Truth & The Life. No one comes to The Father except through Me. If you know me then you know my Father. From now on you do know Him & have seen Him.

John 14:6

A Hidden Soul

We hide out of shame or fear. We hide because no one is safe from the labels that are placed by mankind. But the God that defines everything, knows your soul inside & out and loves you as you are. You shouldn't be in denial or ashamed of who you are or who you've been. You should allow him to Love, Heal & Eliminate, whatever is lifting you up or weighing you down. Human personalities are so different and so complex. There are components of your personality that God intended for you to embrace but also learn from

Personality is a unique style or way of being (Mannerisms, Talents, Hobbies, Interests, Pet Peeves, Sexuality)

God addresses who we are and everything we try to hide. This is a liberating feeling accompanied by the awareness that God's Love is infinite and he makes room for everyone. We are not defined by the world but defined by the Creator of the Universe. In our ability to come out as we are in front of God, we receive healing and peace.

To further grasp this we need to understand that God's nature is to Love and to be Truthful. To be a light in any situation. To be healing where there is brokenness. & to reassure us to avoid fixing what isn't broken. It is an infinite Love that allows us to have compassion for everyone's individual encounter with the Truth. It is a Love that demolishes judgment, pride, ego & shame.

NOTE

1. The Truth isn't subjective or objective. The Truth is Reflective.
2. The Truth Does Not Praise Or Punish.
3. The Truth isn't intended to make one feel superior or inferior.

In a subjective state, the truth is based on one's upbringing, social groups & culture just to list a few. In an objective state, the truth is removed from influence but more specifically it is removed from a spiritual influence. When the Truth is reflective it is also spiritual. With God we can obtain a Truth that is reflective of our identities & reflective of what we need in our soul's journey.

God addresses every aspect of our life in detail so that we aren't just calling things "good" or "bad". We are able to make every experience & encounter, a moment of reflection & internalization. This helps us remove what is hindering us, keeping us in close proximity to God's infinite Love.

An Empty Soul

In our lifetime we become dedicated to many things. We dedicate ourselves to achieving goals, obtaining relationships, material wealth, security, validation & pleasure, just to list a few. God desires to give us all these things in our ability to surrender and place his plans above our own.

We can obtain many things in this lifetime and still feel as though we have nothing. Our perceived necessities are usually things that change and are dependent on circumstance.

There are many things that are essential to our survival, but God's Love is the only essential for our soul's revival.

There can be anything missing in your life and God is always the constant. God is always the refuge. God hears your cries & sees every shattered piece of your broken heart. He looks at the way we see ourselves and he disagrees. He looks at the things we think we need and he says I have something better. It is through his powerful love that he makes everything better, everything new. He doesn't just fill the void. The void overflows with his presence, wisdom, hope, love, direction, discipline, & provision. Everything you need God will supply under the faith we place in him.

God's word is living, Therefore, it's an infinite resource to all of our problems and all the voids in our life. When we sit and meditate on God's word, we retain wisdom, unconditional love, and nourishment that sustains us in any and every situation of our life.

With God I Lack Nothing
Psalms 23:1

A Weary Soul

Every challenging circumstance presents itself as a never ending storm or a walk through a dry desert. You can be battling with restless nights and the feelings of defeat and hopelessness. But we are invited to overcome our weariness through God and with God.

There is a true and inevitable promise that God desires to fulfill in each of our lives. A promise to prosper and not harm. A promise to build character and have an everlasting life. The storms of life are rewarding when we are viewing them from God's beautiful intentions. The bible utilizes victories of great leaders and missionaries to reflect what God has in store for every single one of his children.

While weariness can come from circumstances outside of our control, most often we find ourselves weary of our own efforts. Efforts that we place in people, personal goals, & obtaining things we need. One cannot be weary if they haven't put up a fight. One cannot be weary if they didn't place effort in obtaining something they care about.The good news is that God sees the effort and he sees how weary we grow by simply trying. Simply trying to do the right thing, simply trying to forgive, simply trying to be kind, simply trying to be patient. He sees it all and he promises a harvest for all the good seeds we plant even in a dry or stormy season. Therefore...

Moses's journey is a great real example of God's promise and what happens when you tether yourself to that promise. Moses had a mission to help the Israelites escape Egypt and slavery to inherit the promised land. A land flowing with milk & honey. Although this was the promise, it was a journey where the Israelites felt abandoned by God even after their escape from pharaoh. It was a journey that reflects how important it is to have patience, gratitude and faith in God in the middle of being in a desert. Not only is your soul being rewarded with courage and strength but God's promises never fail even if we have to wait longer than we expect. God brought the Isrealites extremely far from where they were but they began to lose faith. We have to remember where God initially took us out from to have continuous gratitude towards him in spite of our weariness. Moses never stopped planting the seeds of faith, hope and trust in God even if his people were weary in that moment. Weariness is temporary just like many of our circumstances because that is God's promise to us.

let us not grow weary of doing good for in due season we will reap, if we do not give up
Galatians 6:9

An Anxious Soul

The idea that we have control over the many unknowns in our life seems very pleasant. Yet it is simply unrealistic. God invites us to cast all our fear onto him because he is the only one aware of everything that will ever occur in our lives. He is the master of time and fate.

Be strong and courageous. Do not be afraid or terrified because of them, for the Lord your God goes with you. He will not leave you or forsake you
Deutoronomy 31:6

Therefore, do not worry about tomorrow, for tomorrow will worry about itself. Each day has enough trouble of its own.
Matthew 6:34

Other Helpful Tools & Resources

1. Prayer
2. Connecting with God & trusted people (friends, family or mentors & therapists) to express any anxiety our anxious thoughts
3. Journaling
4. Breathwork
5. Walk through nature

These are just a few tactics that help replace the feelings of fear and worry through the perspective that God is bigger than all our problems and worries.

Understanding where your anxiety comes from is an important resource in being able to escape it or minimize it. But it is also important to not dwell in anxiety or to be paralyzed by it. Fear is a very counter-productive emotion. Fear can stop you from interacting with others, going after your calling and simply being able to enjoy the gift of life. More specifically, fear of not having control is also very daunting because we will never fully have control of the things we wish we could control. Fear of not having control invites impulsive & manipulative behaviors into one's spirit. Doing anything out of fear can be destructive and it is important to replace that fear with the truths God has spoken over all of our lives.

When anxiety was great within me, your consolation brought me joy
Psalms 94:19

An **Orphaned** Soul

An orphan is a child deprived of his/her biological parents through circumstances of abandonment, death or separation. An orphan is also a child deprived of protection and the advantage of emotional comfort and rest. It is possible to be an orphan with or without knowing one's biological parents. As we come into this world we are assigned people to watch over us, to secure our well being and growth.

You could've grown up with parents who were "too busy" to even ask how you were doing. You could've grown up wondering "who are my parents." or You could've grown up feeling deep resentment towards your parents for anything you might've personally experienced. These circumstances can have one questioning whether they are loved, whether they matter, or whether they are competent enough to continue in their life's journey.

A Father of the fatherless and a judge of the widows, is God in his holy habitation.
-Psalm 68

The good news is that every soul that claims the title of orphan is not seen that way in God's eyes. The Creator of everything, has a claim over your purpose, protection, emotional development & connection to everything else he has created. This goes deeper than biological roots or the state of feeling neglected. It isn't to say that parents aren't important or that being brought up in an environment that cherishes your development isn't valuable. But if these are things you've lacked growing up, there is a way to reclaim the power of being loved and being a child and it is through our Lord Jesus Christ. A bridge between humanity and God that created everything. He will never abandon you or let you down. He claims that you matter and that you have a purpose even if your circumstances may not seem that way. He demonstrated his Love & how much we matter through his sacrifice.

I will not leave you as orphans
John 14:18

Whatever, you feel was taken from you whether that be the right to a safe home, emotional support, or the affirmation that you are loved, God, The Father equips you with an infinite source of love & forgiveness to give even when you feel you haven't received it.

We often dwell in what we didn't receive as children and withdraw from our God ordained capacity to love and give. You might grow up avoiding the topic of family or building a family because it was foreign to you growing up. But when you become the tree that bears the fruit of love, protection and hope, you are no longer bound by the identity of being an orphan. You are the daughter or son of God who can become the light for a person in need of the same revelation.

An Impatient Soul

When we allow impatience to constrain us we start feeding into the lie that God isn't hearing us or that God doesn't love us. You might be waiting for a promise to be fulfilled or an opportunity to strike. But God is the only one that knows best. He knows what to give you and when to give it to you. God knows when the blessings he has for your life will be treasured the most. He knows that if he gives you something in a season where your character might not be fully developed, you can easily lose sight of the blessing. You might find yourself crediting your efforts and not God's love and will for your life. But in God's mysterious ways, he will also allow us to have things we want for us to later realize it's not what we need. There are several things we need to consider while we are waiting on our promised land.

For the revelation awaits an appointed time. It speaks at the end and will not lie. Though it will linger, wait for it; it will certainly come and not delay.
Habakkuk 2:3

How is what I'm praying for fruitful to my life & my walking with God?

How is fruitful to the life of those around me?

Will I be able to maintain this blessing with my current habits and actions?

Is my faith in place to receive this blessing?

Am I humble?

How do I treat others before & after God blesses me?

Who do I credit & give thanks to when the blessing comes?

How has my intimacy/dependency on God changed after he has blessed me? Has it increased or decreased?

In the period that we are waiting, God wants us to reflect and assess our current state to receive what he desires us to have. We also need to remind ourselves that God is good everyday of our life just for being God, creator and lover of our souls. Your faith and love for God shouldn't depend on any circumstance or blessing. It is said that we need to seek his kingdom first and all the things we need will be added as well. (Matthew 6:33) God deserves our thanks in the midst of our waiting. We are also encouraged to live as though the blessing has already arrived. To live in alignment with God's word, faith and discipline. These things will secure the lasting of any blessing God provides.

We often wait for God to bless us first to do the work he asks of us. We say things such as, "I will help others when I have the money to do so." "I will only be able to love when God sends me the right person." "I will start tomorrow." We want God to work around our states of comfort and not our daily necessity for his presence. It is when we understand this that we become witnesses of God's greater plan of our life.

Finally, we need to understand why God chooses to bless anyone. God blesses us to further our faith and belief in him. His timing is divinely perfect. He is always on time!

A Doubtful Soul

There are those that say, "seeing is believing". We live in a world that isn't reliant on faith based works or miracles. We should learn to see life through a spiritual lens, since faith is not by sight.

By faith we understand that the universe was created by the word of God, so that what is seen was not made out of things that are visible.
Hebrews 11;3

There isn't any one individual who hasn't wondered what the meaning of life might be? Who hasn't reflected on the simple fact that they are alive. We are beautifully composed of a Spirit, Soul & Body. Our spirit is our strongest connection to feeling God even if we can't see him. Our body is being sustained in this lifetime through God's infinite mercy And our souls live throughout eternity. Every soul is assigned a spirit and a body. A spirit that guides and drives the desires of our soul and a body that we are assigned to nourish and hold sacred. Our belief & trust in God allows us to have complete harmony with these three elements. God's holy spirit operates in our lives. A spirit that gives us discernment, a drive to help others, inspiration to follow our dreams, A spirit that allows you to love others unconditionally but also with boundaries. The spirit is sacred and when our souls are darkened it is hard to access the fruits of that spirit. God does not ask for much but he desires for us to acknowledge that we are loved. Acknowledgement that God created the Universe and the Earth we live in & that he is in control of everything. This acknowledgment doesn't require academic knowledge. It just requires faith, power & love.

God speaks in infinite ways. God speaks through the creation, through the people surrounding us, through the mercies and blessings that are placed in our paths. God speaks through that talent or skill you have. God speaks through your kindness and through our humble ability to recognize that there is something greater than all humanity. When you wake up in the morning, God is greeting you to his love and to his mercy. When someone smiles at you or displays an act of kindness in the midst of any trial or tribulation, God is showing up for you. There are infinite reasons to believe. And even in the midst of madness, God wins in the end. We must trust him and believe that he has us in the palm of his hand.

A Tempted Soul

We live in an age where there is an overconsumption of information. Increased awareness leads to increased curiosity or temptation. This can happen through the media, social groups, or at home. Either way, our free will permits us to decide what we do with the information we are given. Through a spiritual lens, God desires for our spirits to be lifted through wisdom over intellect.

Everything is permissible but not everything is beneficial
1 Corinthians 10:23

Wisdom is spiritual and it regards the infinite existence of our souls.

Wisdom is knowledge anointed by Love. It portrays Love for God, Love for Oneself & For those around them. It is light and humble. It is also definitive of character & decision. Knowledge without Love is information exposed to potential corruption.

The disciples were wise to follow Jesus as he obtained the Truth & the path paved by light.

The light of the body is the eye, therefore when the eye is clear, the whole body is also full of light, but when the eye is evil the body is full of darkness.
Luke 11:34

Having a clear & truthful vision (God's vision) allows us to obtain the representative forces of light within our hearts. (Love, peace, forgiveness, content, confidence etc). Jesus replenishes and heals our vision so that our bodies and our hearts are filled with that same healing.

How does this pertain to temptation?

When our vision is clouded it is hard for us to see what areas of our life need healing. God encourages us to combat temptation through his living word.

Blessed is the man that endureth temptation for when he is tried he shall receive the crown of life which the Lord has promised to them that love him.
James 1:12

It is written, Man shall not live on bread alone. But by every word that proceeds from the mouth of God.
Matthew 4:4

These declarations are powerful because there is no temptation or desire more fundamental than abiding by the Spirit & God's word.

We convince ourselves heavily that certain desires are a part of enjoying and living a full life. But God equips us with his Love to discern what is not constructive for our life's journey or mission. In addition, we need to understand that God desires the best for us and that includes how we can enjoy life on Earth as well.

An Insecure Soul

Insecurity exists on a spectrum. In the state of being insecure, we find ourselves in bondage with fear, hatred, envy, pride, comparison, & people-pleasing. There are many reasons as to why we experience insecurity. Insecurity is a state of lacking safety, reassurance, confidence, self-love & identity.

Am I now trying to win the approval of human beings, or God? Or am I trying to please people? If I were still trying to please people, I would not be a follower of Christ.
Galatians 1:10

Our souls are not made for oppression. We are oppressed by what other people say & do. We are oppressed by our lack of forgiveness. We are oppressed by pride and our intent to impress or gain the approval of others. But God liberates us from this bondage. His love and companionship will define you in ways that mankind can't. God disregards what has been spoken over your life & provides you with the insight of who you are in his eyes. His love eliminates the desire to compare & impress others. It is the most Secure Foundation in which we stand on.

Stand Fast therefore in the liberty wherewith Christ has made us free and be not entangled again with the yoke of bondage.
Galatians 5:1

A Reaching Soul

We live in a society where everything has to be earned, exchanged, bought and well-deserved. God does not operate this way. His Love is not limited to good deeds, offerings, and perfect church attendance. While these things are essential in receiving the fullness of God, they aren't the basis of receiving God's love.

God's love is infinite. It is a free gift in which we either accept or reject. God is aware that we all need Love even if our individual paths do not point to that desire. God knows that we all need forgiveness & a chance to start over even if we are in a state of complacency and pride. God's Love does not run out or stop existing. We should be grateful and never take the free gift for granted.

Through the acceptance of this Love we reflect to our Creator how marvelous & impactful his Love is. It is Love that guides you into a Life in Abundance. A life that isn't paced on a chase.

Love is patient and kind. Love is not jealous, boastful, proud or rude. It does not demand its own way. It is not irritable, and it keeps no record of being wronged. It does not rejoice about injustice but rejoices whenever the truth wins out. Love never gives up, never loses faith, is always hopeful, and endures through every circumstance.
1 Corinthians 13:4-7

Where God Met Me

Testimony

A soul is born & a story has been written.

God knew my name & gave me a purpose. My life was written with love & intention. In my disbelief I tried to write my own story... but I failed. As God witnessed this, tears were shed.

Where are you going my dear? Who do you say you are in the places you enter? You're self-destructing to prove to others who you aren't. Your cries have reached my heart and I know you need my Love. In your trauma I've determined your triumph. Come back to me and get to know the plans I have for you. Dwell in the infinite Love, I've placed over your soul when you were born.

My pain became a habit. Chaos became my place of comfort. Trauma was my justification.

It became a habit to constantly please others, it became a habit to deprecate my worth. It became a habit to blame & resent. This was the distance I created between me & my celestial Father. This was the gap that Jesus Christ the Son filled.

In my brokenness I was lustful & hooked on other stimulants. I was always saying yes when I wanted to say no. I was filled with vanity. I portrayed an image that wasn't true to how God saw me. But as God transformed me, he never accused me.

"God, I'm tired of doing this to myself."

You don't have to. You have everything you need in my Son. You have everything you need with Me. I have the romance you're chasing, I have the pleasure you're seeking, I have the peace you can rest on. I have forgiven & cleansed the shame off your body. I Love you Forever.

My spirit rejects the oppression I used to walk in. I was blindly & desperately chasing what I could have in a state of stillness & surrender. I surrendered my pride to live harmonically with the Book of Life. A Book that illustrates our relationship with the Most High. A story in which Love & Happy endings are celebrated. It is a true comfort for our Father, our Creator to see us live out Happy endings. To see our souls rest in infinite peace. It is granted to all souls who want it and all souls who find it.

As I look in the mirror I know that I am just a child of God. I am comforted by Love & I am comforted by grace. I move forward and never look back. I fall and get back up. I forgive myself for not having known myself. In the end...

I am yours and you are mine.

Eden

God's dream was unfolding before me
while I chased the disillusion
Before the paradise could reach its peak of glory
Before my eyes could witness the unimaginable
Before my feet could walk on water
Before my days became infinite
Before my pain was non existent
I let Eden escape me through deception

Even then, my Creator handed me the light in
which i'm reminded...

I have everything I need & the dream will
continue to unfold as I trust him & give thanks.

The Sailor & The Sea

The depth of God's heart is felt by the souls who've been submerged in it...

He sailed his boat on small currents.When he felt the wind had taken him too far, he put down his sail. With such determination, the sailor thought of all the things he would see from the shallow spot he was in. Sitting in that spot for hours, the sailor ran his fingers through the water, feeling the tranquility of the sea. But at times the sea would express despair. The sea had felt abandoned before. With all the life it carries, no one has cared to search deeper. The sea felt it was feared by many. The Creator raised it to love all of creation. Yet every sailor who stayed closer to shore missed the profound love that was in store. The sailor kept running his fingers through its waters, and the sea felt a bond forming. But the sailor couldn't bring himself to go any deeper. The sea was fueled by the sailor's fear. Trying to pull him in with larger waves, the sailor's boat moved in. Bombarded by storms and the injured sea, the sailor lost his boat. Gasping for air, for the surface. The sea felt peace, knowing that the sailor is marked with its true, intense love. In his final moments, he drowned in beauty. He saw the unappreciated makings of the Father.

Daydreamer

Loving without Intimacy
Smiling without Feeling
Dreaming without Manifesting
Forgiving without Letting Go

It is my deceptive mind illustrating possibilities without God

As I wait faithfully to see your face
I am raptured by what your doing today
I sing to you as the soul you saved
I am enamored by
Your mercy, favor & grace
Paradise Awaits

I will not Fear
For the Spirit of the Lord is my Spear
Demolishing defeat, collecting sorrowful tears
Orchestrating his True & Perfect will
I accept as my Spirit remains still

Still in Grace
Still in Faith
Still in Peace
Still in Love

A protection from our Father up above

Life gave me decisions

You gave me freedom

The freedom to have joy & wisdom sing in the same
song
The freedom to feel your light within and see it
written in the clouds with the gentleness & power of
your spirit.

I rest in the arms of humility...

Feeling the Pulses of True Love
Wisdom that kisses my lips
Light that fills my womb
Peace that abides in a synchronized dance
My Soul is in the hands of Freedom

You drown out the world and sustain me in the
supernatural

There's a strong poem behind
A warm hug
An honest smile, A melodic song,
There's peace behind my Father's Son
The Son that illuminates the eyes within
& Calms the storms of confusion
It is in the Oneness of his heart that all
colors shine in the dark

Turned the solo into a choir
Where there's 2 or more the love rises higher
Unity is the strongest language that dances off
your tongue
In our differences, your love makes us one

Gave my song a new meaning. Your love is never fleeting. Keeping me in my darkest hours, helps me bloom like a spring flower. Fear that I might lose your comforting touch but all days of my life are marked by your infinite love

Replenished by the Everlasting Fountain
My Spirit, Soul & Body dance over the fire
that awakens
The Soul

I knew God heard me but I didn't know he loved me...

The difference between now and then, is that I accept everything he does as an act of love: a way to place me on the path of abundance. I can wait, I can trust. Every no, leads to someone better than I was. I accept when my time here is up. I see the excellence in my Father's art, no matter how difficult the battles are in my heart.

How perfect you are, Father...

The way you smile down at your children
Cry when they fall
Laugh when they think they know it all
How Tranquil you are in knowing you're
victorious after all

My spirit lives forever by the grace & desire that abides in the Father. Receiving more revelation,inspiration,& dedication to the gift of eternal living. A gift to exchange sorrow for peace, falsity for truth and pain for healing.

You clear a path for me to flourish
Your the foundation of all my courage
My house overflows with your purity
Purity that is as sweet as honey
Held together by your true love & wisdom
The True Husband

He preserves my words and actions
In silence, I am guided by the truth hidden
behind my pride

You set my mind on abundance. What seemed pleasurable for the moment, no longer satisfies my soul. I am righteously pursuing the paradise painted by your hands. The euphoria spoken by your lips. The world can't imitate the vastness you hold within.

Divine is my Father
Who sees me in ways that I can't see myself
Touched by a grace that makes the heart melt
Who handed me the gift of the everlasting
Calling me to be his even as this life is passing
Who set my eyes on the heavens above
A Father that casts all fear to replace it with
power & love.

I laid there in the pit
not knowing if I was going to make it out
Not knowing I was loved enough to keep going
It wasn't I that dug the pit
But the lies surrounding my heart that made me feel
incompetent
There you are with a hand ready to pull me out
To show me a world beyond fear & doubt
To show me life that is filled with peace, love & hope
To revive my spirit & broken bones

You lived to capture my heart

You died to see my spirit elevate

You came back for more infinite Love

You always were & continue to be

Jehovah Jireh

Elisabet Concepcion has been writing since she was a teenager. She is also a musician, who hopes to help others through her passions. She graduated from University Heights High School and is currently a college student studying English Literature. Her top three hobbies consist of writing, (poetry and music) singing, and serving at her local church. The year of 2023 was challenging for her mental health, being admitted to the hospital due to burnout and stress. This prompted her to realize how important it is to prioritize self-care. She has vowed to continue to create goals for herself in spite of her challenges. Elisabet plans to write more books in the future.

To continue following Elisabet's career, visit her writing page on instagram @venusian.waters.